Besties in the Battle

Cancer and Friendship Colliding

Sandra M. Smith

KWE Publishing

Smith, Sandra M. *Besties in the Battle: Cancer and Friendship Colliding*
Copyright © 2024 by Sandra M. Smith all rights reserved.
ISBN: 979-8-3304-5576-8 (paperback)
Library of Congress Catalog Number: 2024922456

Cover design by Amaya Rose.

Published by KWE Publishing, kwepub.com.

Contents

I dedicate this book to my bestie, Regina Yvette Blagmon.
Our friendship story and cancer battles will be an instrument of
overcoming for others in similar situations.
This book is for those who have been diagnosed with cancer and for their
dear friends who will be with them in the battle.
I pray you will be strengthened with everything you need as you go
through this time. You are worth the fight!

"And we know that all things work together for good to them that love
God, to them who are the called according to his purpose."
Romans 8:28 (KJV)

Testimonial

Besties in the Battle tugs at the heart. A best friend is to be forever treasured. The author and her bestie enjoy and endure a covenant friendship. Both battled against painstaking cancer diagnoses. Readers are given a chance to reflect on their own friendship goals, triumphs, testing of faith, redemption, and loss.

This genuine testament offers self-help tips on engaging with friends, realistic health suggestions and additional scripture references to lead survivors towards a renewed love for life.

–Gwyn R. C. Moses, Ed. D.

Foreword

I had the privilege of meeting the "besties" in the month of April 2015 on a mission trip to Nairobi, Kenya, on the continent of Africa. I happen to wander into their room during our downtime. I listened to their "how-we-became-friends" story.

Before the visit was over, I knew it was much more than a friendship; it was a sisterhood friendship. Two young ladies, who had traveled through life as students, becoming friends, into sister/sistahood, often completing each other's sentences. Laughing at each other's jokes, they sincerely wanted to serve the God that they so loved, and they had the desire to know how to serve Him to the best of their ability. It was a privilege to continue to be a part of their journey.

I was taught by and learned from the besties. It was a blessing to witness how they supported each other through trials and tribulations, in times of joy and accomplishments. When sickness entered the room of their lives, I saw how they fought for each other, even when the other was not feeling well. Their love and kindness toward each other remained and grew. A victory within itself.

Out of the pages of my life story, the besties were and will remain one of my better pages. I am overjoyed to have known and traveled some of the distance with them.

    –Apostle Sheila A. Thompson

Regina and I graduated from VCU in May 2000. When we took this photo, people were commenting about us being twins. Our families didn't know each other yet.

Introduction

Regina and I met in the summer of 1996 on a college campus. Having similar features, we were shorter than most and wore eyeglasses. We were charmingly quiet and internalized much. If you ever had to live on a college campus, daily activity may present a survival of the fittest! We resided at Virginia Commonwealth University (VCU) Rhoads Hall dormitory. Classmates believed we were sisters. She was older than me. We didn't make it a point to tell them otherwise. On the day of graduation, many were still asking if we were sisters, even twins. We stood together, posing for our families. Actually, my bestie was from a town nearly an hour away from my hometown of Richmond, Virginia.

Regina was the truest quiet soul. Jokingly, she was nicknamed "dorm mouse." However, she was involved in multiple social aspects of the university. She presented herself as fun-loving as she was a great dancer. She was a fashionista who loved shoes and color-coordinated outfits. When she stepped out to go anywhere, her accessories and hair pieces matched. She wore the latest hairstyles. I can remember the finger wave scrunches, her hair tightly rolled into a French roll held together with lots of hairpins. I would do a flat twist set for her, too; that was another one of her favorites. My price would set Regina back $5. It was a quiet process between the two of us, but most days, we had company. The other girls would keep the conversation and laughs going.

Unlike myself, Regina was a loud personality on the dance floor. I was the wallflower, just in the building to say I was there. I didn't really enjoy partying, but I would go every time she asked me. We got along so well. We were everywhere together—hanging in the commons, mealtime in the cafeteria, studying in our dorm, and venturing out to the malls. I don't remember any disagreements until years after our college days.

During summer break, we stayed connected through good old-fashioned post mail. My first visit to her hometown of Essex, Virginia, was during a summer break. I drove based on her recited directions that included landmarks to look for along the way. It felt like the longest drive ever on the open road. I grew to love that small town on the Rappahannock River and eating at the Chinese buffet.

Bestie Regina was a country gal with an interest in redeveloping her family's property. We shared tips and tricks for replanting backyard gardens. I chopped kitchen scraps to bury in soil. Compost added nutrients to the soil and helped the vegetables grow bigger. I learned how to hand-pollinate my squash to increase its harvest. It was basically mating the flowers so they could reproduce. Sometimes, growers would do this when there was a lack of pollinators around. We would share pictures of our progress. She had the biggest vegetables growing out of five-gallon buckets on her back porch. I kept my hands in my garden, pulling weeds and peeking at the blossoms. Regina's gardens grew wild and big. She just watered them, and every now and then, she reaped a harvest.

The long drives seemed to get shorter every year thereafter. I reminisce about the "forget-me-nots," the precious time dedicated to preserving our friendship and recognizing our commonalities. Our endeavors became more of a bonding. Regina and I became educators. We were the youngest siblings in our families. We both were given the middle name Yvette (my name was changed in the early months). On

Christmas of 1987, my dad, a homicide victim, lost his life. On Thanksgiving of 1988, Bestie Regina's dad passed away due to health-related problems. Soon after, Regina acknowledged her relationship with God. We began sharing God's word, prayers, and daily encouragement with others. We were ordained as ministers of the gospel in our individual churches and were accepted by the congregants.

Regina was my big little sister. I was given my first diagnosis of cancer in 2020, and Regina followed with a diagnosis in 2022. Again, our roads met. We knew in order to win, we had to fight. Your situation may be widely different or oddly similar. As my bishop would say, "Eat the fish and leave the bones on the plate." Many attributes can be embraced within this book to help you to cherish time and memories and to consider supportive resolutions.

Initially, I asked my bestie to join me as a co-author. Since then, I received a revelation to pursue the writing of our story. Contextual aspirations poured out of my spirit. I wrote what was being made plain to me in the birthday journal Regina gifted me. I began to visualize forthcomings to share with her, hoping she would have equal excitement. However, during her stint of illness, she was not able to bear the load of writing alongside me. The writing of our book became a personal pursuit. It was always my intention to couple our story. God blessed us with twenty-seven years of friendship. I count myself blessed to have been a part of her life as she was part of mine.

Regina had a color theme for every event, big or small. Regina loved loud colors and fashion statements. Regina loved matching her nails to her outfits and her shoes. She would buy props and do her own photo shoots at home.

Chapter 1

Sitting With the Diagnosis

"Thou wilt keep him in perfect peace, whose mind is stayed on thee:
because he trusted in thee."
Isaiah 26:3 (KJV)

There was nothing that could have prepared me for a cancer diagnosis other than the grace of God. Months before my initial encounter with cancer, I prayed against the disease. I told my bestie I remembered saying, "God can dry up cancer in the body!" "God can remove the diagnoses!"

In all honesty, I really wasn't sure if that was possible. I was praying amiss. I witnessed Regina praying for all manner of illnesses. She believed if God brought it to her mind, it was not for her to ponder over impossibilities. She relinquished her thoughts to dwell in the will of God.

At no time did I think I would ever need the same prayers for myself.

Father's Day of 2020, we were enjoying our family time, grilling and running around outside. Our youngest child, age six, was playing basketball and somehow fell onto my lap. I was seated in a low beach

1

chair. His falling onto me stirred the worst pain. I'd never felt such pain across my abdomen. Immediately, my body curled. The pain was excruciating!

Being my mother's child, I fought that pain for hours, from afternoon to night. During that time, I stretched out on the floor, tossing and turning on all sides in search of comfort. A distant thought came to mind that I may need to seek medical attention. I was raised around strong women who bore physical pain, most in silence. It was beyond obvious that they needed to go to the hospital when they finally decided to go. I didn't want to waste anybody's time on a holiday sitting in the waiting room of a hospital. I expected to sleep it off, and I thought I would feel better in the morning. However, the pain continued to surge.

Next, I began regurgitating food. I even questioned, *How can I be sick? Did I break something on the inside?* For hours, I contended with tossing and turning on the floor, trying to find comfort on a sofa, using the toilet, and rinsing myself off at the sink repeatedly. The pain was incomprehensible.

My mom gently suggested urgent care. She thought it was a ruptured appendix based on her experience. I finally took her advice and headed to the nearest urgent care facility with my husband, Victor. After a consult with the doctor, emergency care was warranted. The assistance I needed was only available at the hospital. We returned to the car and drove another thirty minutes into the night. Upon arrival, I needed a wheelchair because the pain had affected my ability to walk. My husband sat with me in the waiting area without an explanation for what was happening to his wife.

As much as I could muster the energy, I texted Regina about the whole ordeal. She encouraged me to go to the hospital early on. I just didn't want to go.

Now, as I was in the emergency department, balled up in the thin white blanket, body wracked with pain and tired from all the events of the day, she offered prayer. She would send a voice memo prayer, as she did many times before. I put the phone to my ear and listened a few times. She prayed for me to have peace. She prayed the doctors and nurses would know exactly what to do for me. Her prayers calmed my spirit. I knew God heard her before I realized He'd hear me as well.

Victor initially had to stay outside due to protocols regarding the coronavirus disease. All I had was my cell phone. Once I was given a room, he was able to join me. I was given pain medication as we waited for someone to shed light on my situation. We had no idea what was going on. I just wanted to rectify the pain I was feeling. It seemed like hours as I tried to sleep, and I also tried to have a conversation with my husband. We talked about routine things, like what we'd do later in the week, what we needed to do at work, and our plans for vacation.

Regina enjoyed shopping for any- and everything. Of course, she loved a deal. She had a wallet full of coupons and her phone was full of apps for discounts. She would strategically choose stores based on her coupons. She would collect so many shopping bags as she made her way to the city and back home. She liked clothes, mostly. Other than that, she had a thing for purses. She enjoyed yard sales and antique stores. That was where she bought things to sell online. They may have been unique or from a different time period. Sometimes, she bought stuff she was collecting for herself. I think she exhausted her double-door closet, dressers, shelves, and any space under her bed for storage. We joked she could have been on a hoarder show. She didn't want to get rid of anything.

There was a significant moment in late spring 2021 when Regina came to town. She would travel to my city to visit her sisters or shop. We met at a mutual favorite salvage spot, Fresh 2 Frozen. Before this, she had talked about her stomach hurting and checking with doctors. I had never thought "cancer," even with the conversations being on the heels of my first experience with the disease one summer earlier. At this point, I was about six months out from my back-to-back surgeries to remove tumors from my ovary and liver. My scans showed no evidence of disease. I was with my mom, and Regina arrived minutes later. We were doing that thing where you call the other person and look around to see the location they were describing. She walked right up behind us. For the most part, she looked like her usual self. She just looked a few months pregnant. Maybe two or three months. I was sure that wasn't the case. That's not information a bestie would neglect to share.

The first thing she said was, "Feel my stomach."

It felt like the tight heaviness of a growing womb.

No way she was expecting a child.

I felt compelled to rub her stomach in a circular motion. As I moved my hand across one area, it felt very hard like the bottom of an unborn baby's foot. Development of limbs began forming during the first trimester of pregnancy. The area felt abnormal considering the chances of my bestie being pregnant were extremely low. I became overwhelmed with chills! I couldn't release my hand from her belly! I began to pray! I prayed wholeheartedly that God would give revelation about the matter. We both stood staring at each other, searching our faces for an answer.

A second significant moment happened as a new season of summer approached. While we were talking on the phone, Regina divulged that she had received a cancer diagnosis. Looking back, I realize I was the friend who tried to keep the fires out. If Regina got worked up about something, I'd be the voice of reason. On this day, she was thinking out loud about all her doctors' visits and the diagnosis received previously identifying pancreatitis. The medications she was ingesting provided minimal relief for what was believed to be pancreatic cancer. Medical tests were scheduled as doctors sought a resolution for conditions related to her digestive and endocrine systems. I may have been of little comfort to her. I believed she already knew more than I was privy to. She and I were very concerned. The least amount of speculation received from doctors was huge! I began fighting for the both of us!

I tried to make myself believe the battle would not get the best of us.

I regret commenting, "It's not like it is something that is hereditary."

Bestie Regina replied, "My mom died from pancreatic cancer."

Bewildered! How did I miss knowing that?

All my defenses were thrown overboard at that moment. Not only did I not succeed in holding her thoughts captive, but I had also forgotten my bestie's mom passed from the same cancer diagnosis.

How am I late to arrive at that conclusion?

Have I failed in listening somehow to my friend?

I didn't have the words to move on to another conversation. The phone call ended abruptly. In my home, I escaped to the half bath and locked the door. Standing in the dark, I cried my way down to the floor between the toilet and the sink. I cried and prayed for God to fix this. I could not imagine life without Bestie Regina. She was such a good friend. She was faithful to God. She hadn't married or started a family. This wouldn't be fair.

I don't know how long I was in that bathroom crouched in the corner. My family broke through the grief as I heard them calling my name. "SANDRA!" "MOM! "

I was not ready to respond.

I remained in darkness, sulking. All the while, I knew when I got up from the pitted place between the toilet and the sink, I would have to deal with the sudden turning of a health crisis. With every excruciating pain endured, I believed each battle would be the last. I was very optimistic about beating this disease and getting on with my life. I had been the only one in the battle. Learning my bestie, my close friend, and I would share a poignant journey was altogether a different fight.

What was the likelihood?

Some would say the odds were stacked against us.

I dare not lose my fight!

This is another cross for me!

The words you hear when the doctor shares a diagnosis of cancer or some other serious disease will hit hard, no doubt. It can be even more intense if you have a loved one who experienced, or passed after a battle with a terminal illness. Know that God is with you, and you are never in this battle alone! Take the time to deal with your emotions through the phases of cancer or any claimed terminal illness. Allow yourself time to hear the medical claim or new information. Whether it is your diagnosis or someone who is dear to your heart, talk to God. Listen for His response. God will guide you into every path that is needed: which doctors to see, what treatments to use, education about the particular diagnosis, and how to share the information with your family, to name a few. Go with God. Our friend and spiritual mentor, Sheila, shared with me, "Don't let any voice speak louder to you than the voice of God." He will not steer you wrong.

My birthday party in 2020, before either of us had been diagnosed with cancer.

Chapter 2

Be Your Strongest Self

"Know ye not that your body is the temple of the Holy Ghost which is in you, which ye have of God, and ye are not your own? For ye are bought with a price: therefore, glorify God in your body, and in your spirit, which are God's."
1 Cor. 6:19–20 (KJV)

The Bible talks about our bodies being a temple for God to dwell within each individual. A desirable standard I consider is for my temple to be strong, clean, and holy unto God. Just as you want a nice place to abide—clean, sturdy, fresh, bright, and peaceful with amenities of choice—consider HIS entrance into a sanctified space for the mind, body, and soul.

My oncologist explained ways to optimize health when not afforded opportunities for chemotherapy or radiation. I have learned there are strengths in various aspects of our health. He focused on four themes: exercise, food, sleep, and stress. He labeled the combination as "Pillars of Health" that activate one's immune system. A healthy body is said to be a strong defense against disease. To become one's strongest self requires building up health defenses.

Pillars of Health

1. Exercise: Move your body daily.
2. Eating: Ingest healthy food.
3. Stress: Control your anxieties.
4. Sleep: Monitor your quality of rest.

Exercise

Consider adding a half hour of walking or other exercise to your day. After one of my surgeries, I would dance to a few songs every day. It was great for my energy level; even if I sat in a chair and bopped around, that activity enhanced my good mood.

Another tip from my oncologist was to think of exercise as the fun thing you like to do. Get moving! Call yourself to it by its name. Instead of saying, "I am going to exercise," you can say, "I am going to dance," or, "I am going to ride my bike." Transcend the activity into purposeful fun.

Speaking of fun, remember the fun of being a kid? During the pandemic, I, like many others, returned to biking since childhood. Bestie Regina had not learned how to ride a bike during her childhood years! However, I knew her to be ready for any adventures. I offered her one of my bikes and began giving her bike lessons. I believed I was qualified to teach her how to ride a bike on her own; I have helped several children learn to ride.

We would go to her uncle's land, and I would push her around in the lumpy grass. I'd ride so she could see how it was done. I was a perfect bike-riding model. I would have her give it a try and run behind her just in case she fell. I didn't want her to have a bad experience. Teaching my bestie to ride increased my level of activity. I remember being soaked in sweat after lessons. We were just like big kids out in the countryside without a care.

Eating

Understand, what goes in will come out. No matter the diagnosis, exercising and eating healthy can be a balm for the body. I suggest larger proportions of fresh fruits and vegetables. Prepare meats by baking more often and prepping with less fatty products. Drink one more cup of water. Lessen sugar by choosing to save desserts for a special day of the week. Do one more thing each day that will lead to healthy eating habits.

Stress

Managing stress presents a bit of trial and error. Think about what relaxes you. Is it alpha waves or the sound of a babbling brook? Is it a serene massage or cuddling with your spouse? I enjoy painting on canvas. I don't consider myself an expert. The colors and creativity are soothing for me. I also love techniques that increase visualization and breathing exercises. I found it useful to meet with someone to guide me through that act of meditating. The chosen facilitator led me to envision myself in particular environments. He talked me through suggestive relaxation techniques and scenarios for the best outcomes. The sessions would prepare me for upcoming surgeries. As I meditated, seeing myself in relaxing places like a beach, for instance, I would say positive statements like, "The medical staff are experienced with my type of surgery, and they will take great care of me."

I learned from my therapist to take deep breaths. It helps to move good energies through the body. For myself, it was more effective to visualize a situation wherein this would occur more freely. My favorite was to visualize a birthday cake. Who doesn't love a birthday celebration? I would envision the warm glow of candles and people surrounding the table where I sat. I would then take a deep breath to blow out my candles. Sometimes, you know, it takes a few times to get all the candles. So, I'd huff and puff until I got them all. This visualization just tickled me. It seemed I'd have these little "birthday parties" every week. The feeling of celebrating another birthday and blowing out the candles made me feel awesome. I would instantly feel happier and less stressed.

Sleep

Once you've relaxed, it may be easier to get quality sleep. I have noticed when I am not feeling my best self or am anxious, my sleep is not the best. My dreams become wonky, and I wake up more often during the night. The body regenerates while we sleep. Naps aren't out of the question. However, a good night's sleep of up to eight hours or more offers health benefits. Identify the best hours and the length of time you can commit to resting. Take time to set your sleep atmosphere. If the room is too warm you will eventually get hot during your rest. So, set the temperature in the room to a cooler setting. Keep the space in and around your bed clear from clutter. Plan relaxing, quieting activities to help you wind down in the last hour or so before bedtime. The brain is able to re-energize. The best sleeping patterns decrease hormones that initiate anxiousness or stress.

One More Pillar...Faith

"Thou art my hiding place and my shield: I hope in thy word."
Psalms 119:114 (KJV)

The noted "Pillars of Health" are likened to sturdy pillars that hold up a building. The stronger your pillars are when combined, the more your physical body will be able to sustain healthy conditions. I am adding this pillar not mentioned by my oncologist. That would be faith and spirituality. Yes, the other pillars could give you peace and help you to feel good about yourself. However, spiritual health is important. In my faith walk, spiritual health is perceived as prayer, scripture reading, and joining a faith community. I give God all the glory and credit for my life experiences. Praying allows my requests to be made known to God. Praise increases my faith in believing God's omnipotent power exceeds all. I regularly read biblical scriptures to feed my soul. I learn from applying scripture to my daily walk with Christ. I search for answers in parables. I pray about everything! I know God hears me and will answer in His sovereign way.

Also, my church family is vital to me. I gain so much within my soul from worshiping and learning alongside other members. I enjoy participating in lively activities beyond the church walls. If this pillar was weakened, my overall health would definitely decline in some manner, and I may find myself regressing in my livelihood.

Faith and spirituality are like muscles. You want your muscles to be firm, powerful. My husband talks about how you have to exercise even when you don't want to because it conditions the body. Our faith needs to be conditioned so that in any situation, it will be strong. It will be built up, ready for any work that needs to be done to benefit the entire body.

Regina and I stopped by the Governor's mansion while riding Segways. I was nervous because she didn't know how to ride a bike. I thought it would be hard for her, but she rocked it.

Chapter 3

Show Yourself Friendly

We can have friends in different pockets of our lives, like church, work, or in the neighborhood. Regina and I began our friendship in college. Opportunities to bond create friendship. Genuine bonding develops through personal consent. God places or suggests people in our lives who are compatible with our assignment, a bond. Sometimes, it's because you are uniquely similar. Other times, the differences between you and the other person are intriguing, so you find yourself constantly engaging with them.

In our case, Bestie Regina and I had some of both sprinkled into our friendship. I can't remember the first conversations, but I remember her presence. She would often come by my dorm room just to play games on the computer. She was very quiet, and I'd considered myself quiet as well. I remember looking at her, thinking, *We really do look alike*. It was like a self-in-the-mirror moment.

We had so many ideas to share and situations to sort out. It was such a joy in the summer months to receive a letter in the mail, sit in a favorite spot, and read her words several times. She had a few close friends—Crystal, Nichelle, and Rhonda. Again, from different pockets. Regina decided the friendship between her and me would make us "besties." We were best friends because of the time, effort, and secrets we sowed into each other.

It was always fun to hang out with my bestie. I enjoyed visiting Tappahannock and becoming more knowledgeable about her hometown. She called the small Virginia town "the country." When we would drive to her childhood home, you could see the Rappahannock River behind the spacious houses on Highway 17. I always dreamed about living in a home with a wide river flowing past the property. Visiting Tappahannock, we would do normal things like shopping or dining. It seemed she knew everybody in the town. We were always stopping to speak to neighbors, people from her high school, and her childhood friends.

Regina really liked yard sales and antique shops, so we'd make time for those. I love food, so I often planned my trips in order to get to the farmer's market. Some of my favorites were pickled watermelon rind and goat's cheese. Every year, the town held a river festival. There would be crowds in the streets, enjoying food and entertainment. She would walk me to the river's edge where I'd collect oyster shells.

In neighboring Urbanna, there was an oyster festival. We talked about going to this festival for years. I was not big on oysters and didn't see the point. However, we made it to the festival just a few years ago... our one and only time going together. I was supposed to be volunteering for a camp. The child I was assisting suddenly had to leave the weekend-long event. Knowing I was more than halfway to Tappahannock, I plotted to get to Regina's place. She told me the oyster festival was happening, and that sealed the deal.

Expecting to be out in the woods all weekend, I had on very rugged attire. It couldn't stop me. We met up so I could hop in her car, and we headed to Urbanna. There were so many people, we couldn't see the festival. Just a sea of cars. We found a spot to park in a field. During this time, we both were diagnosed with cancer, but you would not have known. We were active and happy. After a bit of a hike to get to the festival, we could hear the fun. The first spectacle was the parade through the main street. Her high school's marching band came down in full force, a wave of purple and gold. Several people greeted and smiled at Regina. A few adults stepped out of the parade to embrace her or make a quick joke. She was popular.

We walked, laughed, and taste-tested goodies and sweet treats along the way. There were all kinds of scents in the air. The classic funnel cakes and cotton candy were smelling so sweet. The savory kettle corn was at every turn. Not being huge fans, we sampled a few oysters. I added a splash of lemon on top of the half shell. I remember trying to like them but ultimately throwing them away. We shared a spicy, gooey cup of crab mac and cheese. That alone made the trip worthwhile. We made our way to the river's edge in Urbanna. It was the same river we typically stopped by in her home-town, Tappahannock, just a few miles down. This was our only time visiting near that point of the Rappahannock. The air was perfect, not too hot...not too cold. We were steps away from the noise of the festival. It was just a peaceful spot where we stood and looked across the wide body of water. Just as in Tappahannock, we stared out reverently and thought about life. (Well, I don't know what Regina would think about, but I would think about life.) We let the water lapping at the bank do the talking. The shore was full of white oyster shells, many of them unbroken. I chose one to take home as a keep-sake. Presently, I keep the shell in my home as a treasured reminder of the day.

I leaned heavily on my bestie.

Often, Bestie Regina would dish out her advice where she'd point out information I had not considered. She did a lot of out-of-the-box thinking. However, if I asked her directly for advice on a subject she believed she had no experience with, she would not give it.

If I probed her for things related to being a mom or a wife, she would quickly remind me she was not in those situations and therefore could not offer me assistance. I trusted her with all of my secrets. I believed she could offer me advice for two reasons. I asked her for it, and I knew she would have a different perspective. I wanted her insight. Regina would not bend on things like that. I would get frustrated with her firmness. I'd wanted to question what kind of friend won't give advice, but I had to respect her boundaries.

Our experiences in relationships were different, but I sought her for answers to many of my questions. I was convinced she was wise beyond her years. In my twenties, I called her to tell her I was done with my current relationship. I just wasn't interested, for whatever reason. I told her I was going to stop talking to the guy and move on. She was very adamant that I should find out if I was pregnant.

Why would I be pregnant?!

But...we all know why someone would be pregnant.

So, I took her advice, just to clean up any loose ends...and also prove to her that I was not pregnant.

I most certainly am pregnant!

How did she know that?!

Can I add a classic line right here? "That's what friends are for."

There were times when one of us would offer advice but the other wouldn't accept it. In particular, Regina came across a boy once. Well, I guess it's more appropriate to say he came across her. They were in line together to register for training. He was new to the area and introduced himself. The boy somehow figured out they were in the same part of town. He quickly circled back to find Regina, but she had left. She had some other friends to tell her, the boy actually came by several times within minutes. She was flattered, but I was skeptical. I tried to explain things I'd read and heard about relationships. She would know I wasn't jealous of this attention. However, she may have felt I was trying to keep something away from her that she wanted. I just didn't feel this was right for her. My perspective was, he's too interested, maybe just looking to have fun.

Regina wanted a serious, long-term, monogamous relationship. Never having seen this boy, I was not getting those vibes. I protested her talking to him every chance I got. I didn't have a good feeling about this possible connection. It could have been her excitement or what I perceived as his eagerness. I may have said something like "Lose his number!" He was too interested considering he had not ever seen her before. Despite my admonishments, she let him into her life. That much I knew, but I didn't know how much she'd let him in. I believed she didn't want to hear my opinion on the subject anymore.

The day came when Regina decided to tell me she had been involved with the boy. I didn't see it coming because I really thought she was not messing with him. I am not sure what happened in their relationship...I don't know if she was forced to do something or if they had an argument that turned violent. I don't have those answers. My feelings were between anger and sorrow. I wanted her to have whatever she desired. I never wanted her to deal with the pain of love being snatched from her heart.

I was special to my bestie, and the feelings between us remained truly mutual. Friendships may hit a rock every now and then. We all flail and triumph in our humanness. There was an incident when my bestie and I had heated exchanges. Sharp words were spoken like a knife. I was shocked! I couldn't believe it when she stopped texting me for a few days.

I liked her nerve!

She was ignoring *ME!!!*

Truth be told, it happened a couple of times before we settled our speaking terms.

I thought about some of the other scenarios, like when we did not agree about God operating in karma or the disagreement on how to handle conflicts in the workplace. The pattern had become familiar to me. Typically, the issue was dating. We bumped heads if I objected in any way. She always did what she wanted, so I am not sure why we had to fuss about it. There was the time when she was involved in a long-distance relationship. She never saw this guy, even when there were clear opportunities for him to visit. I felt he was dragging her along.

In another scenario, she was interested in a man and made herself available to him too easily. She would drive a couple of hours to visit, change her schedule, and make pretty complicated plans to spend time with him. He wasn't doing the same. My bestie and I were baby girls in our families. In addition to my ranting, her older sisters often subjected her to their opinions. Even for me, sometimes opinions of older sisters were not received well. Bestie would become upset, choose to avoid her sisters, and set her mind to refute their offerings. I told her, "I guess I am your sister, Bestie, because I am receiving equal treatment!"

I accepted the honor.

To the sisters, besties, and girlfriends, there will be times when we get it all wrong...even with the best intentions. We may say or do the wrong things. We may push when we should back off. We may squeeze when we should be giving some slack.

Included are suggestions based on what Regina and I experienced. We knew we were cared about. We could feel the love of those around us. The issue is everyone loves and cares for others differently. Many want to share advice, because they care. Some will be "passionate" about a particular course of action and urge you in that direction. However, in being a friend, we have to allow space for freewill. We have to use tact. Regina and I had a conversation about this while she was in the hospi-tal. We were unsettled and even angered by our interactions with family and friends. Begin patiently absorbing the Dos and Don'ts. I suggest reading one section at a time. Try to gradually apply multiple strategies. Begin with using a lens of discovering what lies within your space. Your power to choose will be best for your growth. Be receptive to a "light bulb moment!" Trusting God's grace will allow you to embrace mature choices, well-planned responses, and healthy commu-nications.

"How do you eat an elephant?"

"One bite at a time."

Do...

- *Keep in touch.* Obviously, call, but also use virtual calling, send cards/letters, or schedule a visit. You never know when this will be of the most importance. Emotions and thoughts can change so much in the course of a day. It is good to regularly check in with your friend. If they aren't up for calls or visits, send a text. It will be there when they need it.
- *Find reasons to celebrate.* A successful doctor's visit, healthy numbers, keeping food down, or trying out a new therapy technique. Celebrate the little things. This can give you a chance to get out and literally enjoy life and friendship. Take the trip. Do new things. Enjoy the God-given opportunities. Any day above ground is worth celebrating, and I've learned time is short.
- *Be a gift giver.* This doesn't have to be big. You could send a few groceries, pick up a good book, or bring something that reminded you of them. Friends would give Regina helpful products for dealing with side effects of chemo. We would send fruit and vegetables because she enjoyed eating salads. She received blankets to keep her warm. Also, she would be given massages to help with her discomfort.
- *Be attentive.* A listening ear is wonderful when someone is going through. Just be present for your friend. Let them express their pain or vent about their current state. You don't have to have answers. Just let them get it out. Let this time be about them. Take the information you gained, and use it to plan an activity, decide on a gift, or create an inspiring moment.
- *Pour into them.* Do this with your words. Later in this book, I list some affirmations. Speak these types of things over friends and family. Be one who encourages. Tell them they

are gorgeous. If you notice their clothing or a new style, tell them how great they look! Brag about their good qualities. Tell them how much they mean to you and why you love them so much.

Don't...

- *Take it personally.* A lot is going on in the mind of someone with a cancer diagnosis, as is the case with many other illnesses. They could be angry, irritated, or depressed on any given day. They could be off in their focus. Any of this could cause your loved one to present differently from what you are used to. Most likely, it's not about you.
- *Constantly bring up the illness.* People would love to go back to their "normal" lives. Allow them a break from the illness by treating them as you normally would. Hang out if possible. Share a cup of tea on the porch. Gossip or talk about your favorite shows. Laugh, dance, and enjoy each other's company. Let your friend decide when to talk about the illness. It will come up, I assure you.
- *Push too hard.* Even though Regina and I agreed to fight and keep each other up, sometimes, we had to take a break. There were days we both just vented about our illnesses. Allow space for the down days. Unpack the feelings and try to understand where they are coming from. A day or two is alright. Then, start looking for a way to gently pick your friend back up. My therapist suggested that.
- *Avoid the hard truth.* Depending on the type of cancer, a lot of things can change for a person. Most notably, physical appearances could decline. As a result of chemotherapy, weight loss may be a major side effect. They may not be able to walk as usual. It will be very hard to show up for your friend under these circumstances. This is definitely

where relationships are tested. This is when friends really
need friends.

- *Say the "dumb stuff."* Again, I know we aren't perfect.
  However, give a thought to what you are saying, and who
  you are speaking to. Regina shared the dumb stuff people
  had asked. This could be very frustrating for a person who
  is fighting a health battle. Add a little honey. Be mindful of
  things like, "How long do you have", "What if you die?",
  "It's not as bad as __.", and "You should __./Did you __?"
  Lastly, avoid distasteful hospital/medical humor.
  Ephesians 5:4 says jesting is inconvenient.

Regina attended every graduation ceremony for my daughter from fifth grade through college.

Chapter 4

Develop an Ecosystem

I learned about the ecosystem at some point in my education. It's more of a scientific term, about how organisms work in their environments. The rainforest and the desert are examples of ecosystems. I think of ecosystems as a bubble. They are specific areas where living things survive and hopefully thrive. Certain creatures are built for certain environments. Imagine a polar bear living in the desert. The desert wouldn't be conducive to the polar bear's needs of cold temperatures and icy waters.

This scientific term works well as a metaphor for mankind's supportive, human community. Just as the environment can hurt or heal the animal, the same results can happen within humanity. We all need an ecosystem built for optimal survival. Our ecosystems are the community constructed of people, facilities, and coping mechanisms that we lean on to thrive. It includes people who share supportive concerns for you and your health. Our "bubble" of friends and family who support, enrich, and encourage create a niche. We are fed and developed within one's personal ecosystems. "Survival-of-the-fittest" training takes place by nurturing and strengthening the spirits of one another. When one pours into another, just surviving advances to thriving. I hope by making one environment healthy, it will lead us to healthy environments. It's like adding on as you are decorating a room.

Those who are battling cancer must reach out and select creative ecosystems, communities to share in supporting one's needs. Let's begin with the selection of a medical team who will be providing short or long-term care. At the onset, I encourage praying for God to guide medical professionals who have a genuine concern for your personal specifics, are interested in your personality, and respect you as a whole being throughout the processes in a trying situation. Advocating for yourself is vital. It may be necessary to choose a power of attorney over your possessions. Have someone who is knowledgeable about the law to speak for you as needed. Appoint a friend or relative who can stand in the gap as a guardian angel.

Living with cancer gives you a perspective of being mindful of your time and space. These become even more precious when you are dealing with so much unpredictability. In an effort to preserve them, it may be the case where those who are showing themselves as less than supportive will have to be removed. Be mindful; energy can pool. Petition good energies. Anyone who has intentions to stir nagging, negativity, or poor communications must operate within set boundaries for the sake of your wellness. Give them flowers of affirmation through your actions and deeds during their most challenging days and medical procedures.

Genuine friends are a valuable aspect of the human ecosystem. I leaned on friends from work, church, the neighborhood, prayer circles, and of course, family. God blessed me to have Regina during this time. Not only was she my closest and longest friend, but she would also have a cancer diagnosis. Hence, besties in the battle. We could discuss diagnoses, treatments, feelings, pains, doctors, hospital stays, admissions, decision-making, body awareness, sobriety, mobility, and all manner of the diseases as we experienced trial after trial. I believe Regina may have been more informed than I as she also knew and confided with friends who were in likened battles.

Cancer can get challenging for several reasons. You will navigate a new physical ability in some circumstances. Your mind may wander for better or for worse in a short span of time. It may make you start to think you are going crazy. It may lead you to new communities of people as you seek understanding and education. You may have digestive issues, either due to medication or the symptoms of your particular disease. Financially, there could be a shift in your comfort zone as medical expenses most likely will soar. Finding the words and the actions to get through it may be a strain on you. Be sure to show up for your friend. We need a strong ecosystem in times when we get weak. There are many aspects of an ecosystem varying in roles. I believe if you are here, engaged in this book, you are a caring and supportive person in the life of some in a battle for their health. Give yourself credit for your compassion. Pray for direction in your role in your friend's ecosystem. I'm sure you have a place.

I have tried out several support groups during my cancer journey. This is mostly because depending on the type of cancer, I fit into various groups. There may be groups for women, or there could be a group for people with an active diagnosis. Due to the effects of the coronavirus pandemic, many support groups were virtual. An increase in options would allow for in-person meetings. It is possible to find groups for very specific needs, like being diagnosed with a cancer that has shown up generally, for example. Support groups fluctuate due to each person's needs being different. This could make groups large or small in number. One constant I've found, the groups meet regularly and will always be there when you decide to participate.

At a local hospital in my hometown, there is a place within the hospital for patients with cancer. The staff helps you sort through resources available in the area. You can hang out as long as you want before or between appointments. You have access to a kitchen where you can warm food and have lunch. I would describe it as "a spa hidden in grandma's living room." There is lots of warm and natural lighting to maximize relaxation. It was a safe space where one could meet others dealing with similar diseases. In fact, I met staff who were cancer survivors. I have stopped by to greet others and have conversations. The room has comfy spaces, a lovely aroma, and uplifting music. A therapy dog is available for petting to ease emotions.

The center was birthed out of a teen's vision. Robin first dealt with cancer during her senior year of high school. It was her vision to provide a place where families could be supportive while experiencing their own or loved one's journey with cancer. Robin recounted the many times she and her mom had to leave their home to stay in a hotel miles away while going through cancer treatments. Her father wasn't able to leave home. He had to maintain his source of income for the family. She remembered not having both parents in the state hundreds of miles from her home and feeling alone. Soon after, her vision manifested. She connected with a wealthy couple seeking an opportunity to make an impact on the lives of others. She shared her vision for the center, and they sponsored the effort. The center has been helping people like myself, cancer survivors, for over thirty years.

There were other friendly faces during stays at the hospital. They were encouraging, and spiritually refreshing. Regina and I both enjoyed speaking with chaplains. There is most likely a team of chaplains you can connect with if you are in the hospital. Regina enjoyed the attention. Occasionally, the chaplains would bring small gifts of inspiration or short reading materials. I aspired to be a chaplain, so my conversations were twofold. I asked questions about being in the role of a chaplain in addition to talking about my feelings related to having cancer. After my initial interactions in the emergency department, I was really appreciative of the chaplains stopping by. Chaplains would have conversations, always ending with prayer.

Another way we built our ecosystems was by participating in community activities. We built communities in our houses of worship. My church offers opportunities to learn of God, have fun, and volunteer. Faith-based organizations will give you opportunities to serve others, which can be very rewarding and uplifting. I spent a lot of time at local libraries that offer a wide variety of information sessions, workshops, and meetings. My current favorite is the needlework friends' group. This is a space where I, by choice, don't discuss my medical state. I'm just a newly "hooked" crochet enthusiast, looking to perfect my craft. Similarly, Regina followed her interests. She was passionate about history and connections to her lineage. Being involved in several organizations that provided educational opportunities within selected communities filled much of her time.

My bestie and I chose to receive support from a therapist. The specifics of our sessions were always held as confidential. However, my bestie did mention a few times that therapy proved to be a positive support. I also looked forward to sessions with my therapist. I did not have preconceived notions that would hinder me from talking to mental health professionals. Gaining a therapist was one of the best decisions I have made in regard to dealing with medical and mental concerns.

I sought out professional help when I was overwhelmed after returning to my job as a school counselor from brain surgery, too. I could not figure out the next move as far as how to keep the job I'd worked so long to obtain. I was not getting anywhere when I tried to find answers on my own. My therapist, Annette Cornish, is a woman of faith. We have engaging conversations that are light-hearted and inspiring. We started with what I saw as a major dilemma, but we walked a winding path over time.

Therapy doesn't have to be focused on one-dimensional, drastic events. It's good to know when you are doing well. Annette has helped me to recognize growth towards wellness. The sessions extended to stress management, journaling, and self-love. I use what I learned from her regularly. My therapist helped me to be accountable for the path I've chosen. If I decided I wanted to pursue something, she helped me to chart out a plan and set goals to check my progress. When we came together, she had expectations of me showing I'd progressed. She has helped me to process life experiences such as leaving a job due to a diagnosed disability.

When I accepted it was time to go on disability, I did not feel valued. I started earning my own money at sixteen years old, and I knew no other way to engage in society. It was an upstanding thing to go to work. She helped me to understand my value and realize my life wasn't over because I didn't have a 9 to 5 job. We processed what value was. In my experience, worth is the cost of something in regard to a monetary amount. Generally speaking, a quarter is a quarter; that's what it is worth. Value has a sentiment attached to it, however, so the cost is personal. If I decide my time is valuable and more precious than another person's time, no one can dispute that. So, yes, it may be a quarter, but if it was given to me on a special vacation with my mom, and I have held onto it for decades, it would be more valuable than a quarter, personally.

We have the power to set our own value. My value doesn't come from a job, my health, age, gender, or any other characteristic. I wrote down a quote I came across, which says, "Know your worth, and don't give discounts!" When people ask, "What do you do?", there is a lot more to offer as an answer than a career title. I have a creative mind, and I get to use my hands to make items for others. I am a sister-friend to Regina and a few other ladies. We thrive by being a part of each other's lives. Among other things, I am proud to say I am a mom and wife who loves her family in many ways. I am a child of God who uses the gifts He's given me to bless and minister to others.

BC-7 (Blagmon Crew 7). Regina's siblings support each other in everything. This photo is from her ordination service.

Chapter 5

Carry the Load

A round the time when Regina's diagnosis of pancreatic cancer was made known, I was months away from my third surgery. It was for my first brain tumor. Backing up a bit, Regina spent months attending doctors' appointments where they were bouncing around diagnoses like diabetes, gallstones, and pancreatitis. All of that would eventually be diagnosed as pancreatic cancer, which was spreading to her liver. Again, Regina's mom passed away from pancreatic cancer. She didn't say much about it, but the fact had been stated. My sister had recently lost one of her best friends to pancreatic cancer. It was hard to hear but even more difficult to watch my sister struggle through the relationship. She was very supportive and showed up unconditionally for her friend. Just months earlier, my uncle died from pancreatic cancer. We tried to adapt to the quickly changing lifestyle. Nonetheless, his battle was not quite half a year.

These experiences led me to believe this was a dire situation. This cancer would be aggressive and could spread into other organs like it was already doing. In her case, her doctor suggested medical treatment.

Regina was going to start chemotherapy in November of 2022. I was so unaware, I didn't know this was considered "infusion." She talked about the infusion center, and she would need to plan to be at the hospital for several hours. I wanted to support her, so I told her I'd meet her at the hospital. It was about an hour and a half by car. I believe it was a little less for her.

My head was hurting that morning, which had been the case for a few days. I was taking a prescription medication, believing I had a migraine. Our plan was to meet at the hospital in Kilmarnock. It was an early morning ride, which I usually enjoyed. In order to not be impaired, I held off on my medication so that I could get to the hospital safely. I packed up my car and opened the sunroof with excitement and eagerness to blast some driving music. I like gospel and '90s R&B. Most long drives would include Zhane, Jill Scott, and Erykah Badu. My gratitude for the clear mind and traveling mercies would lead me to classic worship such as William McDowell or Jason Nelson.

The hospital looked to be the size of an urgent care facility. However, from my drive through the parking lot, I could see it included an emergency department and other specialties. There was no parking deck. I could tell patients and staff parked in the same area. Several medical professionals were coming and going from the cars. The waiting area for the infusion center was even smaller than the space of an urgent care. There may have been one or two rows of seats. Regina applied lidocaine, as she had been instructed to the port area just under her collarbone. Soon after, we were called to a room set up for a hospital patient, equipped with a small flat screen, a hospital recliner for me, and a rolling tray. Regina would get to relax in a hospital bed for the chemotherapy session.

"Wow, I didn't know you were going to be in an actual hospital room," I said.

"She said I get a meal, too. Just like being a patient."

"Well, yeah, I guess you are a patient," I said. "What about your doctor? Does he come?"

"He said he would. I will talk to him on camera."

"On camera?!"

Regina nodded, then said, "I hope the food is good. If not, I got snacks in the car."

"You want me to go get them now?"

"Yeah...just in case. They have a cafeteria, too. You can go to the cafeteria," she offered.

"Oh, good. I should eat so I can take my medicine."

"You didn't have to come, Sandra. You got your own problems, gal."

I insisted, "It's okay, I wanted to see what it's like. At least this time, you have a little company."

As usual, I had my journal, and I wanted to take notes for her first session. We didn't know what to expect from this appointment, so I thought I should try to capture whatever information she was given. As the nurse talked, I wrote. As Regina asked questions, I wrote the answers from the medical team. As medication was injected, I wrote the amounts. The chemotherapy didn't have many effects on her during the first visit other than a little queasiness, which Regina was given another medication for. She got pretty tired after that. The plan was that her sister, who lived in Lancaster, would pick her up, and they'd return to pick up the car in a few days.

As evening was settling in, I made my way back to Chesterfield. My head had not stopped hurting. One portion of my drive took me across the Robert Norris Bridge, a two-mile bridge with one lane going each way over the Rappahannock River. I started to clutch my steering wheel, then hug it, as I sat up as close to the windshield as I could. It seemed as if my vision wasn't clear. I had a sense of being too close to the edge. I was nervous that I might drive off the side and into the body of water. I was sure the medication had worn off by then. It was a challenging drive even once I was off the bridge.

I would later learn that fall the migraines were actually a mass in my brain. I had been doing routine scans for two years. I had just been cleared at the end of the summer to have scans only once a year. Due to the scans being "head to midcalf," I believed that included *all* of my head. Actually, the scans only went up to my eyes. The tumor was just above my eyes, pressing up against my occipital lobe, so it had gone undetected. By 2024, I would understand my condition to be neuroen-docrine cancer. NETs (or neuroendocrine tumors) are slow-growing cancers. It would take a much longer time for this type of cancer to spread or affect the activity of any organs. At the time, though, all I knew was I had a tumor in my head.

My bestie and I were having scans and follow-ups in tandem during the fall and winter of 2022. Our conversations changed as a result of our cancers. We started to verbally express our shock and awe of us besties being in the particular health states we each had found ourselves. We called each other just to pray, asking God to heal us and asking for revelations for our medical teams. We didn't have a full understanding of what was going on inside of our bodies. Regina continued on a biweekly schedule of chemotherapy while I prepped for brain surgery. She would spend the two days after chemotherapy at her sister's home to be closer to the infusion center. Sometimes, another sister would take the ride with her and drive her home. At any rate, the process was taxing for her. She would get nauseous and cold. Her energy would decrease substantially. I was told my tumors had no treat-ment and could come back or not...there was no way to be certain.

Regina's first day at the infusion center, November 2022.

Chapter 6

Get Equipped for Battle

"Put on God's whole armor [the armor of a heavy-armed soldier which
God supplies], that you may be able successfully to stand up against
[all] the strategies *and* the deceits of the devil."
Ephesians 6:11 (AMPC)

Y ou should know, there are times when you have what you need
for where you are going. There are other times when you pick it
up as you are heading on your way. We are raised to have certain
strengths. Many of us are encouraged to be tenacious, to persevere, and
to give 110%. Most of us have learned how to roll with the punches as
well. When we get hit with a blow, we look for what is in reach to help
us fight back. We don't easily give up our fight.

As a teen, Regina studied the Bible and prayed for hours. I noticed
her faith was strong the day we met. It was not trendy during our
college years. Regina was unashamed about her love for God. She
enjoyed participating in Christian campus activities, especially the
gospel choir. Several of the girls in our dormitory professed they were
Christians. We traveled together to see the VCU Black Awakening
choir on various occasions.

One evening during our freshman year, there was a high night of praise and song. People were standing, clapping, and singing along with the choir. It reminded me of my church not too far away from campus. I didn't have much experience with other churches. I wasn't prepared for Regina's outward expression of praise. Something in that gospel concert touched her heart. She began to cry out in praise to God. It seems her praises exploded in her expressiveness and adoration of God. She was a shortie, but her leaps were very high! It is unknown to me how she was able to leap so high.

A woman behind our row waved vigorously and hollered, "Hold her hand! Hold her hand!" So, I took her hand. Nervously, I wondered if that was the part where my soul would catch on fire. She continued for a few moments more before sitting. I felt I was successful in some unknown way. It was my first time being so close to someone in spiritual praise. I had never seen a young person rejoice in praising God. Even when her body was weak from cancer, she was still popping up, praising God at her church. She was very light on her feet.

Visiting Africa

In 2011, I read *Write It Down, Make It Happen* by Henriette Anne Klauser, PhD. One of the activities in the book was to write down your goals, or maybe it was your wildest dreams. I remember I wrote big things down. One of the big goals I had was to go to Africa. In writing down your goals, you would be more likely to work toward them. The only thing I knew to do was get a passport. So, I set that in motion. I didn't have a specific country or location. I didn't know how it would happen. In sharing about the book, I told Regina that I wanted to go to Africa. More often than not, she was my road dog, so it was loosely an invitation for her to join me. She was not interested. She had concerns about safety being around people as well as animals. We jokingly talked about it.

About four years later Regina had an opportunity to travel to Africa for a mission trip. In 2015, her pastor and some of the leaders would be visiting Nairobi, Kenya, to minister in the communities. There would be worship services and tours in the slums, as I was told. I was so excited for her; I didn't even think about the big goal I'd written down. A friend of mine, Tania, reminded me and encouraged me to inquire. Regina was a minister in her church. Everyone she mentioned was a minister or pastor. I was a deacon in my church. Nonetheless, I told Regina I was interested, and we contacted her pastor, Bishop Daryl Williams. After a brief conversation, we both were invited to join the ministers in visiting Africa. Getting a passport was already checked off my list. Thankfully, mine had arrived months earlier. Completing vaccinations for traveling was the next major preparatory goal. We had weekly meetings leading up to the trip which included education, motivation, and prayer. Everyone participated. We rotated in leading devotions and praying. Everyone needed to be equipped to serve properly.

The time came when we all met at the airport to take flight across the Atlantic Ocean, a first for me and my bestie. I had not flown since I was a teenager, and here I was the day before my thirty-sixth birthday, going to Africa. Regina was on her first flight ever, as I recall. I'd seen the red soil in recurring dreams. I would get off the plane and bend over, scooping up the soil in my hands.

In addition to the two of us and Bishop Williams, there were three others in attendance. Prophetess Sheila Thompson, who would become close to my heart, was also from Regina's church. Another pastor from Maryland and a minister from Alabama were present. We stood and circled for prayer before making our way to the Transportation Security Administration checkpoint. It was a fourteen-hour flight to Kenya. When we arrived, I found the red soil of my dreams, but I did not pick it up. It was right outside of the Nairobi airport in the bright, hot sunshine, just before we reached the car that would take us to our hotel. I remembered, three years earlier, I listed in my journal, "Go to Africa."

The services in Kenya were inspiring, fun, emotional, and moving. Healings took place in the space of what would be praise and worship.

The Kenyans fervently danced on the sanctuary's concrete floors. The congregants would make space around the plastic yard chairs for their praise. We were invited to dance with them. It was an infectious, powerful energy! The men and women danced right next to each other and celebrated God. The Kenyan and Nigerian preachers were passionate and preached with a fire. The American preachers were anointed, as well. I didn't take notes during the messages. At those times, I was focused on the environment. In Africa, people more often walked to the altar randomly for prayer and even discussion. I remember it being hard to give my full attention to any speaker because of the amount of activity taking place.

Regina had the opportunity to preach in Kenya. She was awesome. We could see God was using her. The preachers had to pace themselves because everything had to be translated into Swahili for the attendees. Regina flowed so well. She'd had no experience with preaching alongside a translator, but you wouldn't know it. She prepared her message and had it written out. When it was time for her to speak, she stood up with a member of the Kenyan church. She would speak a sentence or two. Then he would translate that to Swahili. It was a very rhythmic session. The English speakers were excited. Swahili speakers were excited. The sermon went seamlessly. As a deacon, I did not engage in prayers during the altar call when I was in the U.S. However, in Kenya, as the Spirit moved, I was in the midst of the altar and was moved to pray with the ministers.

As ministers laid hands on the congregants to pray, people were falling to their knees, lifting their hands, and even laying out on the concrete slab floor. I remember one woman lying near me. When I went to pray, I reached my hand in her direction, there was a heat radiating from her, something I had experienced only once before at the church my uncle pastors in New York. I remember as a child feeling the fervency of prayer on the altar as my aunt prayed for me. She would stretch her hands over a particular area that needed healing. I had a pain in my eye on that occasion. When she stretched her hand and began to pray, I felt only the area of my eye become warm.

The experience in Africa is always on my mind. The songs I heard are in my spirit. The language of Swahili, the children I saw running around, and the slums we visited are all in my spirit. I became connected to new American friends by visiting Africa. I learned not to miss any opportunities. Speaking up and making your requests known may put you in amazing places. Regina and I gained an understanding of the needs of Kenya. Some were similar to America—the need for education, faith, and community. However, the area of Kenya we visited needed money to feed families. They lacked materials for building homes. The team put together was able to assist in some provisions while we were visiting. I saw and experienced another culture loving God. They loved to praise and sing. God is important to them.

Visiting Minnesota

Our last bestie trip was to visit the Mall of America in Bloomington, Minnesota. Regina pretty much planned this trip independently. I was already out of work, and she offered to pay for my plane ticket. She said she would pay for the room since she wanted to go anyway. I was responsible for my own food and souvenirs. Regina always made provisions for me. She was very generous, especially if she perceived a need. As she saw it, I wouldn't have been able to pay for the trip. I had hospital bills and limited income as a college student. This is literally what she told me when she offered to pay. I tried to explain how I could get it done, but I really could have benefited from someone else taking care of the bill. So, I accepted and was grateful for the opportunity.

We traveled to Minnesota in August. We arrived at the airport in the darkest hours of the morning. Everything was going smoothly with our bags checked and getting through the security clearances, even up to boarding the plane. I was praying all the while. We sat for several minutes before the captain came on the intercom and updated us about something not being in working order with the plane's battery charger. It could take minutes or it could take hours. Regina strategically planned our plane trip to maximize our day. She started to get frustrated. There I was, the mental security, trying to offer all the rationale and positive words to keep her afloat.

She'd say, "This is going to take away our time! We were supposed to have the whole day."

I would politely sing, "It will be okaaaaaaaaaaaay. We have all day tomorrooooooooow. We are going to get there right when we need to be."

To be fair, I was not aware of her plans, so I was still just happy to be on my way somewhere.

It turned out, the battery charger issue would take hours. We disembarked and accepted our complimentary coffee and snacks. As even more time passed, we were afforded a voucher to enjoy breakfast while we continued to wait. We chose a simple breakfast shop that served bacon, egg, and cheese on toast and other tasty entrees to start the day. Regina usually chose a great deal of food and always had something to pack in her bag for later. She ate things that made me nervous because I felt they weren't healthy. At another time, we discussed diabetes and how foods could affect the condition depending on the person's choices. So, I was always very observant of her salt and sugar intakes.

We arrived in Minnesota and enjoyed ourselves for a few days, before heading back home. Upon leaving, we comfortably enjoyed the hotel's breakfast buffet and then made our way to the late-morning flight. Regina didn't eat much. She faithfully attended to her normal routine of checking her blood sugar levels. On the return flight, our one layover landed us in Philadelphia. I was determined to find an infamous Philly cheesesteak. We'd always try new food items together. It was just another special part of our friendship. I offered to buy her a cheesesteak. Sadly, for the first time, she didn't accept. I'd offered to pay for other meals over the course of this trip, but she refused. I ate half of my cheesesteak and saved half.

The final flight of our trip was uneventful. Regina seemed to be tired from all the traveling, so I kept myself busy to allow her time to rest. We didn't have much conversation. She appeared to be resting well whenever I gave a quick glimpse in her direction. That quickly changed!

As the plane ascended to land, all of a sudden, Regina began vomiting. She was seated in the middle of the row seats. Fortunately, the passenger seated next to her slept through the entire episode. Thank God! Everything flowed out of her without a sound. She began to purge onto everything that was seated in front of her, one item being a sorority travel bag that was loaded with personal belongings. I threw my blanket over the bag, thinking it would save the bag from being destroyed. Then, I sacrificed my partially eaten bag of wavy chips! My rationale was that she could use the bag since it was disposable. Just as the plane landed and came to a stop, the vomiting stopped. This incident became another one of those times when we had no words.

Is this related to cancer?

We both knew it was. What else could we do? We stuffed everything into the bag and blanket. Nothing made it to the seats or the floor. However, we had a mess on our hands. We were holding onto a new level in our friendship. We'd never had to clean each other. I felt sorry for her, and I wanted to fix the messiness.

She doesn't eat much. She doesn't eat much at all.

In the airport bathroom, we were met with a rush of women, making the normal pee stop, after a long flight. We outlasted them. Regina cleaned herself up, and we washed soiled items. The makeshift vessel of a blanket couldn't be cleaned in a bathroom sink. It was just too messy and unsanitary. The only resolve was to contain the blanket until we could get home. We rolled it into itself and packed it away in order to head to the car.

Once we returned to my house, I washed everything! I believe she was heading to another event the next day. We never discussed what happened or how she felt. It wasn't that we were pretending it didn't happen. I think it was our acceptance that it was part of her fight.

In our battles, Regina and I wholeheartedly had to rely on God. As church leaders, we pressed the importance of using praise as a weapon. We shared scriptures, prayed over scriptures, and read scriptures over each other's life. Some were repeated, and many scriptures became our daily bread.

The word of God is alive and powerful. Hide the scriptures in your heart, so when you have need of them, God can bring them back to your remembrance. Choose numerous scriptures and post them in strategic places. Rewrite them, and include your name where applicable. I found it powerful to add my name or Regina's name. Psalms 37:4 would be written similar to this:

"Sandra will delight herself in the Lord, and He shall give Sandra the desires of her heart."

Spiritually connect scripture to the healing process. Focus on knowing God is in control. God knows about your infirmities. Pray and search the scriptures to see where God speaks to your heart. Equip yourself for battle.

God Is In Control

Eccl. 3:11 (KJV): "He hath made every thing beautiful in his time: also he hath set the world in their heart, so that no man can find out the work that God maketh from the beginning to the end."

Isaiah 43:19 (KJV): "Behold, I will do a new thing; now it shall spring forth; shall ye not know it? I will even make a way in the wilderness, and rivers in the desert."

Jeremiah 1:5 (AMPC): "Before I formed you in the womb I knew you [and approved of you as My chosen instrument], And before you were born I consecrated you [to Myself as My own]..."

God Is Taking Care of You

Psalm 91:16 (KJV): "With long life will I satisfy him, and shew him my salvation."
(I would read or listen to Psalm 91 in its entirety.)

Isaiah 41:10 (AMPC): "Fear thou not; for I *am* with thee: be not dismayed; for I *am* thy God: I will strengthen thee; yea, I will help thee; yea, I will uphold thee with the right hand of my righteousness."

Isaiah 49:16 (AMPC): "Indeed, I have inscribed [a picture of] you on the palms of My hands; Your city walls [Zion] are continually before Me."

Luke 12:6-7 (AMPC): "Are not five sparrows sold for two pennies? And [yet] not one of them is forgotten or uncared for in the presence of God. But [even] the very hairs of your head are all numbered. Do not be struck with fear or seized with alarm; you are of greater worth than many [flocks] of sparrows."

God Cares When You Are Sick

Isaiah 40:29 (AMPC): "He gives power to the faint, and to him who has no might he increases strength."

John 11:4 (KJV): "When Jesus heard that, he said, This sickness is not unto death, but for the glory of God, that the Son of God might be glorified thereby."

2 Cor. 12:9 (KJV): "And he said unto me, My grace is sufficient for thee: for my strength is made perfect in weakness. Most gladly therefore will I rather glory in my infirmities, that the power of Christ may rest upon me."

James 5:14–15 (KJV): "Is any sick among you? let him call for the elders of the church; and let them pray over him, anointing him with oil in the name of the Lord; and the prayer of faith shall save the sick, and the Lord shall raise him up; and if he have committed sins, they shall be forgiven him."

Use this time to think about scriptures that speak to your heart and situation.

"I love to pose." She took her first ride (as a passenger) on a motorcycle that day.

Chapter 7

Speak Life

"I shall not die, but live, and declare the works of the LORD."
Psalm 118:17 (KJV)

Ahuge part of getting through something as challenging as a serious diagnosis is building yourself up. Affirmations are positive words spoken over yourself or another person. Positive self-talk is a simple strategy for combating a poor sense of self-value. Your value does not come from your diagnosis, your physical abilities, or your current circumstances. So, build up your affirmations. They are very useful when you find yourself doubting who you are or worrying about what will be. Scripture says, "As a man thinketh in his heart, so is he" (Proverbs 23:7). Our thoughts are powerful. Many times we need to win in our mind to be successful with what's in front of us. Just as with scripture, we can take quotes or things we've heard and use them to boost ourselves at any time. Also, just as we pray for one another, we can affirm our friends who may be dealing with an illness.

This is where faith comes into play. It's the basis of what we hope for. It's the proof of what we don't see with our natural eye. We can have faith based on what God has already done. We can have hope for what will be. We build ourselves up by feeding our spirit with positive words. You have to find your value. God has assigned it to us. The way you see yourself creates a reality. Find it in the word of God. Learn what God says about you. Your worth is in the word. The value God has placed on you is the value you should place on yourself.

The Bible says we are adopted. God adopted us. Think about how costly of a process it is to go through an adoption. There is a lot of time involved. There can be thousands of dollars connected to an adoption. Yet God still considered us worthy. That's how God loves us. We are that valuable to Him. He thought we were worth saving. And nothing can separate us from His love. The cost doesn't come from our condition, and the value doesn't come from our view. We are valued and worthy because God has declared us so.

It may help to forgive yourself, accept yourself, and be there for yourself before getting into the affirmations. Two keys to this are to watch your criticism of yourself and speak kindly about yourself. James 3:10 says, "Out of the same mouth come *both* blessing and cursing. These things should not be." We have a moral obligation to speak in a manner that reflects our fear of God and profound respect for His precepts. Decrease the negative self-talk, which is saying things like, "It's all my fault..." or "It's really over now..." It's listening only to the bad parts or seeing things as either super bad or absolutely perfect. Instead, increase the positive self-talk. Positive self-talk encourages you.

These affirmations are from a wide range of people, some famous, some I know personally. Some came out of conversations with my bestie. They are mind-shifters to help fight against our "stinking thinking," as my bishop would say. These are statements I speak over my family and friends—even strangers when appropriate.

Words of Affirmation

I am a believer and a fighter.

I am more than a conqueror.

I expect a miracle.

I am a walking miracle.

God's favor is over my life.

All things are working together for my good.

I can change the narrative.

My home is a peaceful dwelling place.

God has me.

Jesus loves me.

Giving up is easy; I can do hard things.

Look how far I've come.

Jesus is my help.

I can do this.

It will get better.

I am healthy.

"I will live a long, healthy, prosperous, anointed life." –Pastor John F. Hannah

Nothing is produced without a struggle.

"There's nothing in the caterpillar that tells you it will be a butter-fly." –R. Buckminster Fuller

Regina enjoyed trying new things: squishing grapes, zip-lining, riding the donkey, and canoeing.

Chapter 8

Let God Be Sovereign

I heard in my spirit, "sovereign." Basically, sovereign means God is king. He is solely in charge, and it's whatever He says. That's tough to allow sometimes. I've been in the place to question God, unfortunately. However, as I say often, if God be God, and He is sovereign in my life, it's what He allows. This is where we have to give our cares to God, and then get up from that care.

In the Bible, David is grieving the possible loss of a child with Bathsheba. He was truly hurt, and he was calling out to God while fasting. The people were concerned for David as he was sorely broken. They didn't know what was going to happen to him. However, after some time, the child did pass. It was at that time David rose and went on with living. No doubt, the people were left baffled. As David explained, "We don't know how God will be gracious to us."

I went through a traumatic few weeks during the fall of 2023 because I couldn't understand God not answering my prayers as I requested. The doctors decided chemotherapy was no longer useful for Regina. I felt we were losing the spiritual fight. I wasn't sure how long she'd be with me. But I refuse to believe cancer is bigger than God. I can't see God showing the world cancer can win. I was thinking, *I must be missing something in this equation.* My friend had been back and forth in the hospital. In my current state, I couldn't drive to be with her. Something was happening to my physical body, and I was in so much pain.

Regina's challenges were also growing. One day, she shared with me that chemotherapy wasn't helping any longer. The doctor suggested she meet with hospice. Literally the next day, I learned I had a fourth tumor and would need to have surgery. That was my second brain tumor in eleven months. All of this sent me into a depression. It was a lot hitting me at once, hitting us, with no control on my end. Regina told me she didn't know what else to think. I was praying constantly. Many people were praying for her. We were praying the same prayers. "This sickness is not unto death. You shall live and not die." I was scared...scared of what would happen if I stopped praying and scared of what would happen if God didn't move as I felt I needed.

My close friend and one of my "peeps," Tania, helped me to know this was not because of anything we did. God had the ultimate say. We are only to trust in God, accepting what He allows. Empower yourself today by accepting God as sovereign. Trust Him to take the best care of the entire situation. Release the cares. It's said, "If it's out of your hands, it deserves to be free from your heart." It's God's. He will work it out for good in the end.

After this conversation, while I sat at home, I surrendered Regina's battle to God. Surrendering is handing something over and releasing your control of it. In my circumstance, this was not quitting. I did not give up on Regina. I continued to pray and be there as much as I could for her. I just loosened my grip and placed her in God's hands. I had been clinging to our long friendship. I had a firm grip on her being healed and getting back to doing what she loved. I would pray and then I'd squeeze so tight, like a bear hug, to Regina's situation. I was asking God to help, but I was not *giving it to Him* so that He could. Imagine if you asked someone to fix your car, but you never gave them the car. They aren't going to be able to help you much if you won't release it. That's where I was, wanting help but not trusting the Helper. When I made a conscious effort to surrender the outcome to God, I began to experience more peace. A weight was lifted from my shoulders as time went on.

I had not seen Regina for about a month when she said she would come to visit. She'd been in and out of the hospital while I had been under-going surgery for my second brain tumor. The last time I visited her had been maybe a month earlier, at the hospital. I had Tania drop me off, and my mom would pick me up after a few hours. We both were in pain, and we vented to each other for the first part of the visit. One of the nurses thought it was so "awesome" that we had cancer in common. She literally used the word, awesome. Regina enjoyed sharing our friendship and how we had so many things similar between the two of us. She proceeded to share with the nurse. It was a conversation to prepare the nurse for Regina's closing statement. Regina made sure to let her know, "We got plenty of things in common. Cancer doesn't have to be one of them!"

We planned to have our visit on December 12th, a Tuesday. I was excited and anxious in the days leading up to it. I began praying for the visit. I wanted to enjoy our time. I wanted her to be comfortable. I wanted to cook for her. I wanted the house freshly cleaned to avoid her picking up any germs. I had taken up crocheting, so I made gifts for her and her sister.

She arrived with her sister that afternoon. I stood at the door, waiting to hug her. I knew she'd been through a lot. I knew it was a challenge for either of us to reach each other, but I had no idea. I was not prepared for what I would see. It took her some time to get herself together. When she did, she reached her hands out of the vehicle. They were thin. Frail. This is often an image that comes to mind out of the blue when I think of her to this day. I immediately had a sinking feeling in my stomach. I felt a lump in my throat, and I held back tears. I had a talk with myself as she continued to descend from the truck. *Get your-*

self together. This is your friend! She did not come here for you to break down and cry in front of her. Don't make her feel worse. Get it together! Suck it up. Whatever you are feeling can wait until this visit is over. Get excited to see your bestie. So that's what I did.

I cheered as she made her way into the house. The visit was tough. Regina tossed and turned, fought to keep food down, and tried to explain her life as it was at the time. We conversed about a few things. I explained she could leave whenever she wanted. I was just glad she had come. Her sister said she was bound and determined. We prayed as they'd been doing daily for some time.

Shortly after the prayer, I told Regina I saw her in the Spirit, holding onto a rope. She wasn't fighting or struggling as we discussed. We had agreed we would fight. We would keep each other off the ropes. Also, she wasn't giving up. She was concerned about quitting when her fight was getting harder. I told her I saw her holding on tight with both hands. God was saying, "Hold on. You don't have to fight, and you aren't giving up."

She and her sister prepared to go home. Just as she had come, she took her time making it back to the truck, her sister guiding her carefully. The walk seemed to be exhausting, and she had to sit to catch her breath. I reached into the cab of the truck to hug her, and we instantly started to cry. Praying even more for God to help my friend, I hugged her. I was physically holding her too tight. I had to let her go because I was causing her discomfort. I tried, so I released my embrace and held her hands. I did not want to let go. We held hands and cried a moment longer while her sister offered us encouragement.

I thank God for that visit. Regina left this side of heaven some hours later. I was told she spent her last night lying next to two of her sisters, having lots of conversation. During Regina's funeral, I shared:

"Regina and I were besties. There is a quote that says, 'Friends are the family we choose.' I was called her sister before I ever met her. We were at VCU together, and people would ask if I had a sister on campus. The girl in question turned out to be Regina. She introduced me to so much: Essex and the Rappahannock River; ministry and mission work. I

traveled with her to several states and even abroad to Kenya. Every trip left me with more meaning for my life and our friendship. I want to share two things with the rest of the two fishes and five loaves...that's a scripture reference Regina would use to describe her siblings:

"Psalm 24:1 says, 'The earth is the LORD's, and the fulness thereof; the world, and they that dwell therein.'

"God is sovereign.

"Psalm 37:23 says, 'The steps of a good man are ordered by the LORD: And he delighteth in his way.'

"Accept what He allows. Regardless of how this feels to us, God knows what He's doing."

This is one of my favorite pictures of Regina. We were attending a wedding. She matched the wedding colors perfectly. The dress fit her perfectly. We had fun dancing and eating.

Chapter 9

"My Heart Will Go On"

I had a dream once. Regina was bound about her neck with a metal collar, similar to what a slave may have been placed in when captured. It was a thick, dark-colored yoke. She was sweating, and her tongue was hanging out of her mouth. She had lost her hair except for a few patches. Her face was swollen, maybe from the pressure under the collar. I was next to her, encouraging her to remove it, but she would not. There was no explanation of why she wouldn't do so. I had the sense that she was capable of taking it off, and that made me frustrated. She seemed to be ignoring the fact that she was in this distressed state and just sat there, suffering under the literal chokehold of the collar.

I woke up and wrote down all the details of the dream so I could share it with her. I was very concerned to share a dream with Regina. Mainly because the dream made me think she was suicidal. I thought God was showing me she would harm herself. This was several years ahead of our cancer battles. As I had done in many instances, I was trying to protect her from harm. I wrestled with sharing for that reason. After some days, I did mention it to her. We were having lunch at one of her local spots. I brought the journal I used to write the dream down.

We decided Regina was under a great deal of stress or pressure, and it was choking her, adding to her anxiety. She told me her hair was thinning, and she wondered if it was stress. She was worried about several family members and some other issues at the time. I admitted my relief because I was thinking she was going to harm herself. She told me it was so much, and things were hard, but she didn't confess to any thought of harming herself. The image of her being choked by that collar is always in my head. It drove me to check on Regina often, to know where her head was and if she was feeling overwhelmed. Pay attention to your thoughts and dreams. Sometimes, God uses them to direct you to reach out to your loved ones.

In the days after Regina passed, I had kind of a recurring dream. It wasn't the exact same dream every time, but it was the same idea. She was easing away from me. In the beginning, I would see her hands. We were tightly holding hands. Each night, the grip loosened. After a while, I could see Regina and I were in close proximity, enjoying each other's company. These were what I called *"The Color Purple"* dreams. In the film, two sisters have a magnetic bond that cannot be broken, no matter the trials they experience. However, I could tell with each passing night that Regina was moving away.

In my waking hours, I was worried I would forget her. For some reason, I thought I'd forget all of our fun times and conversations and what I learned from her.

The dreams went on for several more nights. She'd be in the dream over in the distance, almost as a bystander. Then the hand dreams returned, and her face was visible. These were what I called the *"Titanic"* dreams. The story reaches a point where the lovers are shipwrecked, holding onto a piece of wood in the ocean. In order to save herself, the woman has to push her love off of the wood they'd been clinging to. Regina and I would be holding hands across a wooden board, and she was always in the water. The setting always seemed like night. She was calm, and I was not afraid. I had a sense that this was something we had to do. Nightly, the hold loosened. While awake, I knew this was another form of me surrendering her to God. There was a night I dreamed our hands were on the board but not touching. The final night, I saw Regina drift away as I held on to the board. The last image in my dream was her hands washing away in the ocean. I have not had dreams of her since that time. She is still with me in my thoughts every day.

Please don't think Regina lost this battle. She lived a wonderful life full of service, love, vitality, and courage. There were many things she sought to do, and many of them she accomplished. She wasn't one of those to let, as they say, the grass grow under her feet. She had always been surrounded by friends and her loving family. She was a faithful leader in her church. She took on this fight with everything she had. It was an inspiration to be in her circle and see how she pressed through the effects of cancer in her daily activities. She was a walking testimony of God's goodness.

As for the things she desired in her heart, like starting a family of her own, I cannot be upset about them not coming to pass. In my opinion, she was well-deserving of the things she wanted. However, I trust God to be our sovereign God. Everything happens for a reason. Regina touched so many people, known and unknown. I once invited her to pray in the park while we were serving people in the community. She poured into those strangers so powerfully! People we had never seen and would never see again. She was mighty in God. She trusted Him with her life, and she did her best to live to please Him.

This book, *Besties in the Battle*, was definitely my dream, but I fully expected my bestie to help me write it. I started writing with a big concern that I'd forget her, but I remember Regina daily. She is with me when I see brightly colored suitcases. She loved to travel, and I had planned to buy her a suitcase for her birthday. I see her when I see other ladies dressed in vibrant colors or with intricate nail designs. Regina was certain to coordinate her outfits and nails. I think of her when I hear the names of places we visited, like Dallas and Minnesota. She was always seeking to learn new things, so I think of her when I am met with new ideas or challenges.

Upon her passing, it became my goal to find ways to keep her memory alive. She has most certainly helped me write this book as the memories and conversations were recalled. I would want anyone who has read this to know I loved Regina. My hope is she is pleased with how I have presented her through this work.

Citations

"A Quote by R. Buckminster Fuller." Goodreads. Accessed September 18, 2024. https://www.goodreads.com/quotes/38044-there-is-nothing-in-a-caterpillar-that-tells-you-it-s.

Cameron, James, dir. *Titanic*. 1997; United States: Paramount Pictures.

Dion, Céline, "My Heart Will Go On," *Titanic: Music From the Motion Picture*, Sony Classical, 1997.

Klauser, Henriette. *Write It Down, Make It Happen: Knowing What You Want and Getting It*. New York City: Scribner, 2000.

Mall of America is a trademark of MOAC Mall Holdings LLC.

Segway is a trademark of Segway Inc.

Spielberg, Steven, dir. *The Color Purple*. 1985; United States:

Acknowledgments

I thank God for life, health, and strength. I am extremely humbled and grateful to be among the living and able to capture memories and perspectives for *Besties in the Battle*.

I extend thank-yous to my church family, Children of God Victory Tabernacle, for their support during rough seasons of diagnoses and surgeries. Your kindness and prayers were invigorating and restorative. Special thanks to Bishop M. Louis Lacey, who planted seeds of wisdom into my spirit decades ago that continue to be blessings today.

Thank you to my husband, Victor, for unselfishly being with me through the cancer journey. We could write our own book. Thank you for your support as I processed my friendships, questioned my directions, and began to work toward finding myself during this season. Thank you for accepting my responsibilities and demonstrating grace as I wrote at all times of the day. You are a great defender and motivator. I love you dearly.

To our children, Xavier, Zofia, Isabella, and Amaya, I thank you all for your suggestions and encouragement. Amaya, I know I ran you every which way, but thank you for your artistic ability in designing the cover for *Besties in the Battle*. Isabella and Zofia, I appreciate your enthusiasm for my projects. Thank you for your concern for me. Xavier, thank you for understanding the importance of my friendship with "Godmommy Regina." Thank you for simplifying what I would perceive as complicated.

Thank you to my mom, Virginia, for always telling me I could be an author. I believed you. I'm grateful for your example of serving others, despite your own challenges. I consider how you care for people when I have the opportunity to serve. I am impressed by your generous heart.

A special thank you to my therapist, Annette Cornish. She came into my life at the onset of a collision. I felt like my world was crumbling and found myself in a dark place with no direction. Meeting with you helped me mentally to find ground to stand on moving forward. Our sessions strengthened me. Thank you for helping me to find my way to a healthy place.

Dr. Gwyn R. C. Moses, thank you for spending time with me as I took on this new project. I see you as a shining example of support in the community and using your God-given creativity. Thank you for your mentorship and for agreeing to work with me as a first-time author.

A special thank you to the Blagmon family. I appreciate your family's support and genuine hospitality throughout our friendship.

Dr. Michael Pyles, Sheila Thompson, and Vinata Washington, I appreciate your support as the first readers who helped me to organize my thoughts into literature.

About the Author

Sandra M. Smith is an educator with experience in the areas of exceptional education and school counseling. She is a graduate of Virginia Commonwealth University, in her hometown, Richmond, Virginia. VCU is where she met her bestie, Regina Blagmon. Sandra is a neuroendocrine cancer survivor who wants to help others make the most beneficial moves toward winning against cancer and  other serious diseases. Sandra founded the Regina Blagmon Memorial Scholarship with financial support from the Blagmon family and contributors. She serves as a minister at the Children of God Victory Tabernacle. She lives in Chesterfield County, Virginia, with her husband and children. She loves watching documentaries and cooking at home in her kitchen. Her most recent interest is crocheting. *Besties in the Battle* is Sandra's first book.

Printed in the USA
CPSIA information can be obtained
at www.ICGtesting.com
LVHW051759301124
798014LV00001B/209